The Sainsbury Book of
CAKE ICING & DECORATING
Carole Handslip

CONTENTS

Published exclusively for
J. Sainsbury Limited
Stamford Street, London SE1 9LL
by Cathay Books
59 Grosvenor Street, London W1

First published 1981
Reprinted 1982, 1983, 1984

© Cathay Books 1981
ISBN 0 86178 068 X

Printed in Hong Kong

INTRODUCTION

Cake decorating is a fascinating and rewarding craft. This handbook shows you just how simple it can be, and encourages those of you who have the basic skills to try something more elaborate.

Beginning with simple butter icings, each chapter takes you step-by-step through icing techniques, progressing to designing and royal icing a wedding cake. Each chapter provides a selection of cake recipes, using the techniques described within the chapter.

Step-by-step photographs show you how to make a variety of cake decorations, including piped flowers, chocolate shapes, marzipan fruits and Christmas cake decorations. Many of these decorations can be prepared in advance and stored until required – to avoid a last minute rush.

Some of the cakes – especially the royal iced ones and more elaborate novelty cakes – take time to complete but you will find this absorbing hobby satisfying. By practising the techniques in each chapter and following the suggested designs you should be able to produce a professional cake for every occasion.

NOTES

Standard spoon measurements are used in all recipes
1 tablespoon = one 15 ml spoon
1 teaspoon = one 5 ml spoon
All spoon measures are level.

Ovens should be preheated to the specified temperature.

For all recipes, quantities are given in both metric and imperial measures. Follow either set but not a mixture of both, because they are not inter-changeable.

Recipes for the basic cake mixtures, almond paste and royal icing (marked with asterisks) are given in the reference section (pages 86-91).

Eggs used in the recipes are standard size, i.e. size 3, unless otherwise stated. If large eggs are specified, use size 1.

Basic Decorating Equipment

You will probably find that you already have most of the basic equipment needed for simple cake decorating.

Several *mixing bowls* and *small basins* are needed when working with different coloured icings.

A *sieve* is necessary for sifting icing sugar to ensure that there are no lumps in the icing.

A *spatula* enables you to scrape every last bit of icing out of a bowl and avoids wastage.

A small and a medium sized *palette knife* are a great help when spreading icing over the top of the cake and round the sides.

Piping nozzles for simple icings are usually larger than those used for royal icing. A 5 mm (¼ inch) and a 1 cm (½ inch) 8-cut rose nozzle will probably be sufficient for use with butter icings. A No. 2 writing nozzle is useful for piping glacé icing and melted chocolate.

Nylon piping bags are necessary for piping butter icings.

Greaseproof paper piping bags are best for piping melted chocolate and glacé icing.

Fine paintbrushes are used for painting food colourings onto icings and moulded decorations.

A *sugar thermometer* is essential when making American frosting and fondant icings. Stand it in hot water for a few minutes before and after use. Clean and dry thoroughly.

A *cake board*, or a thinner *cake card*, enhances an iced cake but is not essential; a large flat plate can be used if liked. Cake boards and cards may be used again: just wipe them over with a damp cloth and leave to dry – do not wash them.

As you become more interested and wish to achieve better results, there are additional pieces of equipment that will help you. These are described in the chapter on royal icing.

To Make a Greaseproof Paper Piping Bag

A greaseproof paper piping bag is the simplest to use for royal icing. Make several at a time if you are using different piping nozzles or several colourings, or icing a large cake.

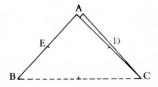

1. Fold a 25 cm (10 inch) square of greaseproof paper in half to form a triangle.

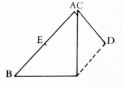

2. Fold point C to point A on a flat surface and crease well.

3. Fold point D over to point E and crease well.

4. Fold point A to point B and crease well.

5. Hold the bag where points D and E meet. Shape into a cone, overlap points twice and crease to secure.

6. Cut off the tip of the cone and insert a nozzle. Do not fill more than half full.

SIMPLE ICINGS & DECORATIONS

Cake decorating can be as simple as sprinkling icing sugar onto a cake through a d'oyley or strips of paper. Glacé icing the top of a cake and applying bought sweets or other decorations when dry is another simple idea.

The sides of a cake can be left plain but they look more attractive if covered with butter icing or apricot glaze and then rolled in toasted or coloured coconut, nuts, or a similar coating. If the sides are coated, decorate the top edge of the cake with smarties, chocolate drops, or nuts to finish it off neatly. For a more decorative finish, pipe butter icing around the edge.

Individual cup cakes are quick to make and easy to decorate effectively. Top them with glacé icing, then apply sweets, nuts or cherries and angelica, or mark a feather design on the icing (see page 15).

Glacé Icing

250 g (8 oz) icing sugar
2 tablespoons warm water (approximately)
flavouring (see below) or few drops of food colouring (optional)

Sift the icing sugar into a mixing bowl and gradually add the water. The icing should be thick enough to coat the back of the spoon thickly. Add the flavouring or colouring and use immediately.

This quantity is sufficient to ice 18 to 24 small cakes. A half-quantity will ice the top of a 20 cm (8 inch) round cake.

Makes a 250 g (8 oz) mixture

FLAVOURINGS

Coffee: Replace 1 tablespoon warm water with 1 tablespoon coffee essence.

Orange or lemon: Replace 1 tablespoon warm water with 1 tablespoon orange or lemon juice. Add the grated rind of 1 orange or lemon and a few drops of food colouring.

Chocolate: Sift 3 tablespoons cocoa with the icing sugar.

Crème au Beurre

2 egg whites
125 g (4 oz) icing sugar, sifted
125 g (4 oz) unsalted butter
flavouring (see below) or few drops of food colouring (optional)

Place the egg whites and icing sugar in a mixing bowl over a pan of simmering water and whisk until the mixture holds its shape. Cool slightly. Cream the butter until soft then beat in the meringue mixture a little at a time. Flavour or colour as desired.

This quantity is sufficient to fill and ice the top of a 20 cm (8 inch) sandwich cake.

If stored in an airtight container, this icing can be kept in the refrigerator for several weeks.

Makes a 125 g (4 oz) mixture

FLAVOURINGS

Chocolate: Melt 50 g (2 oz) plain chocolate in a bowl over a pan of hot water. Cool and beat in with the meringue mixture.

Coffee: Add 1 tablespoon coffee essence with the meringue mixture.

Praline: Add 3 tablespoons crushed Praline (see page 14) with the meringue mixture.

Butter Icing

125 g (4 oz) butter
250 g (8 oz) icing
 sugar, sifted
2 tablespoons milk
flavouring (see
 below) or few
 drops of food
 colouring
 (optional)

Beat the butter with half the icing sugar until smooth. Add remaining icing sugar with the milk and flavouring. Beat until creamy.

This quantity is sufficient to fill and cover a 20 cm (8 inch) sandwich cake.

If stored in an airtight container, this icing can be kept in the refrigerator for several weeks.

Makes a 250 g (8 oz) mixture

FLAVOURINGS

Lemon or orange: Add the grated rind of 1 lemon or orange to the butter. Replace the milk with lemon or orange juice. Add a few drops of yellow or orange colouring.

Mocha: Blend 1 teaspoon cocoa powder and 2 teaspoons instant coffee powder with 1 tablespoon boiling water. Cool, then add to the mixture with only 1 tablespoon milk.

Chocolate: Blend 2 tablespoons cocoa powder with 2 tablespoons boiling water. Cool, then add to the mixture with only 1 tablespoon milk.

Coffee: Replace 1 tablespoon milk with 1 tablespoon coffee essence.

American Frosting

250 g (8 oz)
  granulated sugar
4 tablespoons water
pinch of cream of
  tartar
1 egg white

Put the sugar and water in a heavy-based pan and heat gently, stirring occasionally, until dissolved.

Add the cream of tartar and bring to the boil without stirring. Boil for 10 minutes or until the syrup registers 115°C (240°F) on a sugar thermometer.

Meanwhile, whisk the egg white until very stiff. Pour the sugar syrup in a thin stream onto the egg white, whisking all the time. Continue to whisk until the frosting stands in stiff peaks, with the tips just falling.

Spoon the icing onto the centre of the cake and spread over the top and sides, working quickly as the icing soon starts to set. Form into swirls or peaks with a palette knife.

Place any decorations in position while the icing is still soft. The icing forms a crisp crust but remains soft underneath.

This quantity is sufficient to cover an 18 cm (7 inch) round cake.

Makes a 250 g (8 oz) mixture

Caramel Frosting

175 g (6 oz) soft
  brown sugar
1 egg white
2 tablespoons hot
  water
pinch of cream of
  tartar

Put all the ingredients in a bowl over a pan of hot water and whisk for 5 to 7 minutes until thick. Use immediately, forming into swirls on the cake with a palette knife.

This quantity is sufficient to fill and cover a 20 cm (8 inch) round cake.

Makes a 175 g (6 oz) mixture

VARIATION

Mock Frosting: Replace the brown sugar with caster sugar. This can be used as a substitute for American frosting if you do not have a sugar thermometer.

Chocolate Fudge Icing

50 g (2 oz) butter
3 tablespoons milk
250 g (8 oz) icing
 sugar, sifted
2 tablespoons cocoa
 powder, sifted

Melt the butter in a small saucepan with the milk. Add the icing sugar and cocoa and beat well until smooth and glossy. Leave until lukewarm, then pour over the cake.

This quantity is sufficient to fill and ice the top of a 20 cm (8 inch) sandwich cake.

Makes a 250 g (8 oz) mixture

NOTE: If the icing is too thick to pour, reheat gently to thin.

13

SIMPLE DECORATIONS

To decorate the sides: Apply a layer of butter icing, or brush with apricot glaze.

To make apricot glaze: Place 250 g (8 oz) apricot jam and 3 tablespoons water in a small pan and heat until dissolved. Add a squeeze of lemon juice, then sieve and return to the pan. Bring to the boil and simmer until syrupy. Use warm. The glaze can be stored in the refrigerator for several months; reheat gently to use.

To apply the coating: Place on a sheet of grease-proof paper. Hold cake between the palms of the hands and roll lightly in the coating until evenly covered. Grated chocolate, crushed corn-flakes, hundreds and thousands, and chocolate strands are simple but effective. Chopped or flaked nuts, coloured or toasted desiccated coconut and crushed praline are also good. Flaked or chopped almonds are best toasted.

To toast coconut or almonds: Place on a baking sheet under a moderate grill for a few minutes, stirring frequently, until golden.

To colour coconut: Add a drop of food colouring and stir until evenly coloured.

Crushed praline: Gently heat 50 g (2 oz) each unblanched almonds and sugar in a small pan until the sugar browns and the almonds begin to split. Turn onto an oiled baking sheet to cool. Crush with a rolling pin. This can be stored in an airtight container for several weeks.

To decorate the top: Effective finishes can be created using butter icing or other icing with suitable texture.

1. Draw a palette knife across the icing from side to side, slightly overlapping the previous line each time (see page 23).

2. Spread a thick layer of icing over the top of the cake. Pull up into peaks with a palette knife (see page 13).

3. Using a palette knife, make swirls all round the cake, from the outside to the centre (see page 11).

4. Using a fork make a circular design all around the cake, then draw a pointed knife from the edge towards the centre in 8 places to give a scalloped effect.

Feather Icing

This gives a professional finish to glacé iced cakes. It is essential to work quickly before the icing begins to set.

Place the cake on a wire rack. Pour three-quarters of the glacé icing onto the centre of the cake and spread almost to the edge with a palette knife. Give the cake 2 or 3 sharp bangs on the table to help the icing flow to the edge. If icing drips over the edge, quickly remove with a knife or leave until set and trim. Place cake on a board.

Colour the remaining icing, spoon into a greaseproof paper piping bag fitted with a No. 1 writing nozzle. Pipe parallel lines 2.5 cm (1 inch) apart on the glacé icing.

Working quickly, draw a pointed knife vertically across the icing alternately in opposite directions at 2.5 cm

(1 inch) intervals to make a feather pattern.

Do not move the cake until the icing is set, or it may crack.

Circular Feather Design: Pipe a continuous circle on a round glacé iced cake, keeping the rings about 2.5 cm (1 inch) apart, using the contrasting colour. Draw a pointed knife from the edge to the centre, at regular intervals to create a scalloped effect.

Painted Feather Design: Onto the glacé iced cake, paint parallel lines, using food colouring and a fine paintbrush. Draw a knife across the icing alternately in opposite directions.

Simple finishes

The finishing touches can turn a simply iced cake into something special. Chocolate drops, orange and lemon slices, smarties, jelly sweets and silver balls make very attractive edgings. Whole hazelnuts and walnuts are equally effective; if the top icing is chocolate, sprinkle walnuts with icing sugar to make them white before placing them on the cake. Glacé fruits, crystallized violets and rose leaves, and sugar flowers can also be bought for finishing decorations.

If you have time, make your own decorations. Frosted fruits make a pretty home-made finish to a simple cake. Caramel chips are especially good used with caramel frosting.

A more elaborate edging can be achieved by piping butter icing into borders, rosettes or shells.

To make caramel chips: Place 175 g (6 oz) caster sugar in a small pan and heat gently until dissolved. Boil until it forms a golden caramel, then pour immediately onto a greased baking sheet and leave to cool. Break into pieces.

Frosted Fruits, Flowers and Leaves

These are quite easy to make and look most attractive. They are also edible. Frosted fruits will keep for up to 2 weeks, leaves and flowers may be kept for up to 6 weeks. Store between layers of tissue paper in an airtight container.

Small fruits such as currants, grapes and cherries are the most suitable.

Flowers with only a few petals, such as primroses, violets, campanula or rose petals, give the best results. Only use edible ones.

Leaves should be small, preferably a herb, such as mint, which also has a pleasant flavour.

Simple Frosting Method

This can be used for fruits, flowers and leaves.

1 egg white
fruit, flowers or leaves
caster sugar

Lightly whisk the egg white. Using a paint brush, lightly coat the fruit, flowers or leaves all over with the egg white. Drain or brush off any excess. Dip or dredge in caster sugar until well coated all over. Place on greaseproof paper to dry.

Gum Arabic Method

This method is not suitable for fruit.

15 g (½ oz) gum arabic
2 tablespoons rose water
flowers or leaves
caster sugar

Place the gum arabic and rose water in a screw-top jar and shake well. Leave for 2 to 3 hours, shaking occasionally, until the gum arabic has dissolved.

Paint all over the petals or leaves, covering completely. Place on greaseproof paper and leave overnight until the solution has been absorbed. Sprinkle both sides of the flower or leaf with caster sugar; shake off any surplus. Sprinkle again if necessary then leave on greaseproof paper to dry.

Chocolate Mint Cake

4-egg chocolate
  Victoria sandwich
  cake mixture*
peppermint
  flavouring
250 g (8 oz) green
  Butter icing (see
  page 11)
125 g (4 oz) green
  Glacé icing (see
  page 9)
TO DECORATE:
75 g (3 oz) chocolate
  sugar strands
50 g (2 oz) plain
  chocolate, melted

Line and grease two 20 cm (8 inch) sandwich tins. Divide the mixture between the tins and bake in a pre-heated moderate oven, 180°C (350°F), Gas Mark 4, for 25 to 30 minutes. Turn out onto a wire rack to cool.

Mix a few drops of peppermint flavouring into the butter icing. Use half to sandwich the cakes together.

Cover the sides with more icing and roll in the chocolate strands. Place on a cake board.

Put the remaining butter icing in a nylon piping bag fitted with a 5 mm (¼ inch) fluted nozzle and pipe a border around the top of the cake.

Pour the glacé icing onto the top of the cake and spread almost to the edge with a palette knife, being careful not to touch the piping. Gently bang the cake on the table 2 or 3 times to help the icing flow to the edge.

Put the melted chocolate in a greaseproof paper piping bag, cut off the tip and dribble the chocolate across the top of the cake.

Makes one 20 cm (8 inch) cake

Frosted Fruit Cake

3-egg orange-
  flavoured Whisked
  sponge cake
  mixture*
4 tablespoons
  cointreau
450 ml (¾ pint)
  double cream,
  whipped
TO DECORATE:
frosted grapes and
  mint leaves (see
  page 17)

Grease and flour a 23 cm (9 inch) ring mould. Turn the mixture into the tin and bake in a preheated moderately hot oven, 190°C (375°F), Gas Mark 5, for 30 to 35 minutes. Turn out onto a wire rack to cool.

Cut in half and sprinkle with the liqueur. Sandwich together with a quarter of the cream and place on a cake board. Cover the cake with the remaining cream and mark into a swirl pattern with a palette knife.

Arrange the frosted grapes and leaves in clusters around the top.

Makes one 23 cm (9 inch) cake

Coffee and Almond Gâteau

3-egg Whisked
sponge cake
mixture*
250 g (8 oz) coffee
Crème au beurre
(see page 10)
75 g (3 oz) flaked
almonds, toasted

Line and grease a 20 × 30 cm
(8 × 12 inch) Swiss roll tin. Turn the
mixture into the tin and bake in a
preheated moderately hot oven,
190°C (375°F), Gas Mark 5, for 20 to
25 minutes. Turn onto a wire rack to
cool.

Cut the cake into 3 equal pieces
and sandwich together with one
third of the icing. Cover the sides
with more icing and coat with the
almonds. Place on a cake board.

Use a quarter of the remaining
icing to cover the top of the cake,
smoothing with a palette knife. Put
the remaining icing in a nylon piping
bag fitted with a 5 mm (¼ inch)
plain nozzle and pipe lines diagonally
across the top of the gâteau.

Makes one 20 cm (8 inch) gâteau

Spider's Web Cake

4-egg chocolate
  Victoria sandwich
  cake mixture*
125 g (4 oz) coffee
  Butter icing (see
  page 11)
75 g (3 oz) walnuts,
  chopped
2 teaspoons cocoa
  powder
1 teaspoon boiling
  water
250 g (8 oz) coffee
  Glacé icing (see
  page 9)
1 tablespoon sifted
  icing sugar

Grease and line two 20 cm (8 inch) sandwich tins. Divide the mixture evenly between the tins and bake in a preheated moderate oven, 180°C (350°F), Gas Mark 4, for 25 to 30 minutes. Cool on a wire rack.

Sandwich the cakes together with three-quarters of the butter icing. Spread the rest around the side, roll in the nuts and place on a cake board.

Blend the cocoa with the boiling water. Add 3 tablespoons of the glacé icing with the icing sugar and beat well. Spoon into a greaseproof paper piping bag.

Pour the remaining glacé icing onto the top of the cake and spread almost to the edge with a palette knife. Gently bang the cake on the table 2 or 3 times to help the icing flow to the edge.

Snip the tip off the piping bag and pipe a continuous circular line, starting in the centre of the cake and working towards the outside edge.

Quickly draw a pointed knife from the centre to the edge, marking the cake into quarters. Then draw from edge to centre between the lines to complete the pattern.
Makes one 20 cm (8 inch) cake

Lemon Cake

4-egg lemon-
flavoured Whisked
sponge cake
mixture*
6 tablespoons lemon
curd
300 g (10 oz)
yellow Glacé icing
(see page 9)
yellow and orange
food colouring
TO DECORATE:
25 g (1 oz) yellow
desiccated coconut
(see page 14)
sugar flowers

Line and grease a 23 cm (9 inch)
round cake tin. Turn the mixture
into the tin and bake in a preheated
moderately hot oven, 190°C (375°F),
Gas Mark 5, for 30 to 35 minutes.
Turn onto a wire rack to cool.

Cut the cake in half and sandwich
together with 4 tablespoons of the
lemon curd. Spread the remaining
lemon curd around the side of the
cake, then roll in the coloured
coconut. Place on a cake board.

Pour three-quarters of the glacé
icing onto the top of the cake and
spread almost to the edge with a
palette knife. Gently bang the cake
2 or 3 times on the table to help the
icing flow to the edge. Leave to dry.

Colour the remaining icing with a
few more drops of yellow and a drop
of orange colouring. With a No. 2
writing nozzle pipe lines across the
top of the cake. Pipe across the first
lines to form diamonds. Leave to set
then place a flower in each one.
Makes one 23 cm (9 inch) cake

Mocha Gâteau

3-egg coffee-
flavoured Whisked
sponge mixture*
250 g (8 oz)
chocolate Butter
icing (see page 11)
75 g (3 oz) plain
chocolate, grated
chocolate buttons to
decorate

Line and grease a 20 × 30 cm
(8 × 12 inch) Swiss roll tin. Turn the
mixture into the tin and bake in a
preheated moderately hot oven,
190°C (375°F), Gas Mark 5, for 20 to
25 minutes. Cool on a wire rack.

Cut the cake into 3 equal pieces and
sandwich together with one third of
the butter icing. Spread more icing
over the sides, then coat with grated
chocolate. Place on a cake board.

Spread more icing over the top and
mark with a palette knife. Using the
remaining icing and a fluted nozzle,
pipe a border along the edges of the
cake. Top with chocolate buttons.
Makes one 20 cm (8 inch) gâteau

ELABORATE CAKE DECORATING

Having mastered the simple icings, you will probably want to try your hand at something slightly more complicated. It is only practice that will give good results, but once learned, icing is a skill that will always be useful.

The icings given in this chapter are used for covering large and small sponge cakes; they could also be used to cover a rich fruit cake if it is coated with almond paste. The finished icing on sponge cakes will be improved if the cake is first brushed with apricot glaze (see page 14).

Satin and moulding icings are also used to make moulded decorations, which add a really professional touch to the finished cake.

Fondant Icing

150 ml (¼ pint) water

500 g (1 lb) granulated or cube sugar

1 tablespoon liquid glucose

flavouring (see below) or few drops of food colouring (optional)

Heat the water and sugar in a heavy-based pan gently until dissolved. Bring to the boil slowly then add the glucose. Boil until the syrup registers 115°C (240°F) on a sugar thermometer.

When the bubbles subside, pour one third into a bowl and the remainder into a separate bowl. Cool until a skin forms.

Working the smaller quantity first, beat with a wooden spoon until thick and white. It will change from a liquid to a paste and finally to a solid white mass. Knead with the fingers, until smooth.

Shape into pieces, the size of a golf ball. Repeat with the larger quantity of fondant. If stored in an airtight jar, this icing will keep for up to 2 months.

To use, place 3 or 4 pieces in a basin over a pan of hot water. Warm gently, stirring, until the fondant is smooth and the consistency of thick cream. Add flavouring or colouring if using. If the icing is too thick, add a little water.

This quantity is sufficient to cover a 20 cm (8 inch) round cake.

Makes a 500 g (1 lb) mixture

FLAVOURINGS

Coffee: Add 2 teaspoons coffee essence.

Chocolate: Blend 1 tablespoon cocoa with 1 tablespoon boiling water. Cool before adding.

Satin Icing

50 g (2 oz) butter or
    margarine
4 tablespoons lemon
    juice
675 g (1½ lb) icing
    sugar, sifted
    (approximately)
few drops of food
    colouring
    (optional)

Warm the fat and lemon juice in a pan until melted. Add 250 g (8 oz) of the icing sugar and heat gently, stirring, until dissolved. When the mixture begins to simmer at the sides of the pan, increase the heat slightly and cook for 2 minutes until it boils gently; do not overboil at this stage or the icing will be too hard.

Remove from the heat and add 250 g (8 oz) of the icing sugar. Beat thoroughly with a wooden spoon, then turn into a mixing bowl.

Gradually mix in enough of the remaining icing sugar to give a soft dough. Turn onto a surface dusted with icing sugar and knead until smooth, adding colouring if using.

Wrap in cling film. This icing will keep in the refrigerator for up to 6 weeks.

Use to mould decorations or to cover the top and sides of a cake. This quantity is sufficient to cover a 23 cm (9 inch) round cake.

Makes a 675 g (1½ lb) mixture

Moulding Icing

1 egg white
1 rounded tablespoon
*   liquid glucose*
500 g (1 lb) icing
*   sugar, sifted*
*   (approximately)*
few drops of food
*   colouring*
*   (optional)*

Mix the egg white and glucose together in a basin. Gradually add enough icing sugar to form a stiff paste. Turn onto a surface sprinkled with cornflour and knead until smooth.

Wrap in cling film and keep in a plastic bag to prevent it from drying. The icing will keep in the refrigerator for up to 6 weeks. If the icing does become dry, dip it in hot water, wrap and return to the bag for 1 hour then knead again, adding colouring if using.

Use to mould decorations or to cover the top and sides of a cake. This quantity is sufficient to cover a 20 cm (8 inch) round cake.

Makes a 500 g (1 lb) mixture

MOULDED DECORATIONS

Moulding icing is an extremely pliable icing suitable for making flowers and other cake decorations. It holds its shape even when paper thin, and as it is white it is easy to achieve natural colours. Food colourings can be kneaded into the icing or painted on the finished decoration. Keep the icing to be moulded wrapped in a polythene bag as it dries quickly if exposed to air. Leave the decoration for 24 hours to dry and harden.

edges outwards. Repeat, overlapping each petal, until the desired shape is achieved, using a cocktail stick if necessary to help mould the petals. Leave to dry overnight then cut off the base. When using several roses together in a decoration, colour some a shade darker for a more elaborate effect.

Rose

Make a cone with a small piece of icing and press out the base to form a stand. Take a piece of icing the size of a pea, dip in cornflour and roll into a ball in the palm of your hand. Using a hard-boiled egg, flatten the icing in your hand with quick gentle strokes, using more cornflour if it is too sticky. The edges of the petal should be paper thin.

Daisy

Make a small ball of icing and pinch the bottom to form a base. Flatten the ball (as for the rose) to make a thin round. Using small scissors, cut the edges of the round to form petals, then turn them upwards. Using a cocktail stick, make holes in the centre then paint with yellow food colouring. Using pink food colouring and a fine paintbrush, paint the tips of the petals. Leave to dry.

Carefully wrap the petal around the cone, turning the

28

Leaves

Colour the icing green and roll out the icing thinly on a surface dusted with cornflour. Cut into leaf shapes with a small knife. Lift into the palm of your hand, flatten the edges (as for the rose) and pinch each end into a point. Leave to dry overnight.

Mark veins on each leaf, using a fine paintbrush or the point of a knife dipped into colouring.

Rabbit

Mould a piece of icing into an egg shape. Mould a smaller piece into an oval and place on top of the narrow end of the egg shape to form the head. Shape 2 large ears and attach to the head. Shape a small ball of icing for the tail and attach. Paint the inside of the ears with a little pink colouring. Using pink royal icing* and a No. 1 writing nozzle, pipe on the eyes.

Chick

Shape two balls of yellow icing, one half the size of the other. Stick the small ball on top of the large one for the head. Using small scissors, snip the small ball to form a beak shape and paint the mouth with yellow colouring. Position coloured sugar balls for the eyes.

Mouse

Mould a piece of icing into a cone shape for the body. Shape 2 pieces of icing into ears and stick onto the pointed end, which will be the head. Roll a small piece of icing into a thin tail and stick onto the rounded end of the body. Using royal icing* and a No. 1 nozzle, pipe on eyes.

ALMOND PASTE DECORATIONS

Almond paste used for modelling must be supple enough to bend without cracking, but firm enough to hold its shape. Bought ready-made marzipan is ideal to use for making decorations as you can simply break off the amount you need. If using homemade almond paste, make a large quantity and keep it in a polythene bag, breaking off small amounts as you need them; it will keep for several weeks. Care must be taken not to over-knead, as this will make the paste oily and difficult to handle.

To colour the paste, add a little food colouring at a time, kneading in until it is evenly coloured. Keep the paste not being worked in a polythene bag, as it dries out quickly if exposed to air. Leave the decorations for 2 to 3 days to dry before positioning on the cake. Alternatively make up to 4 weeks in advance and store in an airtight tin.

Oranges and Lemons

Colour some paste orange or lemon. Roll into a ball for an orange and a plump oval for a lemon. Roll over the fine surface of a grater to get the texture of the skin. Press in a clove at one end for the calyx.

Bananas

Colour some paste yellow and form into a banana shape. Paint with brown colouring to represent the skin.

Apples

Colour some paste green and roll into a ball, making a slight indent at the top and base. Cut a clove in half and use the top for the calyx and the rest for the stalk. Paint pink colouring on one side, gradually blending it into the green.

Pears

Form some paste into a pear shape. Use a clove for the stem and calyx as for apples. Paint with green and pink colouring, gradually blending in the colours.

Strawberries

Colour some paste red and shape into a rounded cone. Roll over the medium surface of a grater or roll in granulated sugar. Make a hull from a small piece of green coloured paste and press onto the top of the strawberry.

Plums

Colour some paste purple, using pink and blue colourings. Roll into an egg shape and mark a line down one side. Press a clove into the top for the stalk.

Grape Cluster

Colour some paste green or purple (see plums) and shape into a cone. Roll out small balls for the grapes and stick onto the cone. Press in a clove for the stalk.

Carrots

Colour some paste orange and shape into small cones. Make stalks from a small piece of green coloured paste. Press into the carrot tops.

Cabbage

Colour some paste green. Shape about two thirds into a small ball for the heart. Shape the remainder into 6 or 8 leaves. Arrange the leaves around the heart, overlapping each one. Press gently at the base to adhere.

Parsnips

Shape some paste into a cone. Paint with brown colouring and make a stalk from a small piece of green coloured paste.

Peas

Shape tiny pieces of green coloured icing into balls.

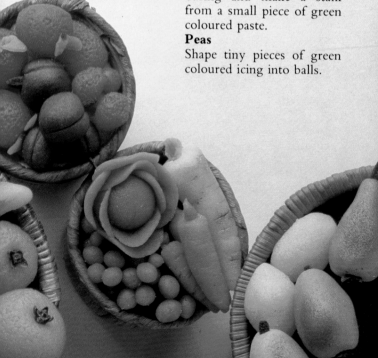

CHRISTMAS DECORATIONS

The following decorations are made with almond paste, with the exception of the Christmas rose which is shaped with moulding icing. Templates for the Christmas tree and star can be traced from the outlines on pages 92-3.

Fir Trees

Colour some almond paste green and some brown. Shape the green into cones and the brown into trunks. Press each cone onto a ball. Mark with a skewer.

Christmas Rose

Cover the top of an essence bottle with foil. Take a piece of moulding icing the size of a pea, dip in cornflour and roll into a ball in the palm of your hand. Place on the foil. Shape a similar piece of icing into a petal, as for Rose (see page 28). Repeat to make 5 petals and pinch onto the ball of icing. Leave to dry.

Remove from the foil and paint the centre yellow with food colouring. Shape a small piece of yellow moulding icing into a ball and place in the centre. Using yellow royal icing* pipe stamens in the centre. Leave to dry.

Christmas Tree

Draw the outline of a Christmas tree on a piece of card, then cut out to make a template. Colour some almond paste green and a smaller piece red. Roll out both pieces evenly. Cut out a tree from the green paste and a tub shape from the red, using the template as a guide. Leave to dry.

Pipe dots of icing on the tree and place coloured sugar balls on top.

Father Christmas

Colour some almond paste red. Shape into a plump cone for the body and a smaller, thinner cone for the hat, allowing the tip to drop over. Hollow out the base of the hat to fit over the head.

Roll some natural coloured paste into a ball for the head and fix onto a cocktail stick. Using white royal icing* and a No. 1 writing nozzle, pipe on eyes, nose, beard, bobble and buttons. Leave to dry, then assemble.

Holly Leaves

Colour some almond paste deep green. Roll out evenly on a piece of waxed paper. Cut into rectangles, then cut each into a holly leaf shape, using the base of an icing nozzle. Mark veins on the leaf with the point of a knife. Leave to dry, laying some over a spoon handle to give a curved shape. Colour a little paste red and roll into tiny balls for berries.

Stars

Make a template of a star (as for Christmas tree). Roll out some natural or coloured almond paste evenly. Cut out stars, using the template as a guide. Leave to dry. Using white royal icing* and a No. 1 writing nozzle, pipe lines round the edges of the stars. Decorate the points with silver balls.

CHOCOLATE DECORATIONS

Chocolate cake covering or plain chocolate gives the best results for decorations. Break into small pieces and place in a basin over a pan of hot water. Heat gently until the chocolate melts, taking care not to let any water get into the chocolate; do not overheat.

Leave the chocolate shapes to dry in a cool place, but not in the refrigerator or they will set with a dull finish. Chocolate shapes can be stored in an airtight container for several weeks.

Handle chocolate decorations carefully because they are delicate. Make more than you require to allow for breakage.

Rose Leaves
Pick fresh, undamaged leaves with clearly marked veins. Wash them thoroughly and dry carefully. Coat the underside of each leaf with melted chocolate, using a fine paintbrush and making sure the chocolate is spread evenly right to the edges.

Allow to set chocolate side up. When hard, carefully lift the tip of the rose leaf and peel away from the chocolate.

Squares, Triangles and Circles
Spread a thin even layer of melted chocolate on a piece of foil or greaseproof paper. Leave until just set, but not too hard.

Cut into squares using a sharp knife and a ruler. To make triangles, cut the squares in half. To make long-sided triangles, cut the chocolate into rectangles, then cut in half. When hard, carefully lift the tip of the paper and peel away from the chocolate. To make circles, cut the chocolate into small rounds, using a pastry cutter.

These shapes may be decorated with a piped chocolate design if desired. Fill a greaseproof paper piping bag with melted chocolate. Snip off the end and pipe straight or zig-zag lines onto the shapes. Leave in a cool place to set.

Chocolate Caraque
Spread a thin layer of melted chocolate onto a marble slab or cold work surface using a palette knife. Leave until just firm but not hard. Using a sharp thin-bladed knife at a slight angle, push the knife across the chocolate with a slight sawing movement, scraping off a thin layer; this will form a long scroll.

Short curls can be made by peeling layers straight from a block of chocolate with a potato peeler. The chocolate must not be too cold or it will not curl satisfactorily.

Valentine Cake

4-egg plain or pink
  Victoria sandwich
  cake mixture*
125 g (4 oz)
  strawberry jam
125 g (4 oz) Apricot
  glaze (see page
  14)
500 g (1 lb) pink
  Satin icing (see
  page 26)
125 g (4 oz) Royal
  icing*
pink moulded roses
  (see page 28) to
  decorate

Line and grease a 20 cm (8 inch)
heart-shaped cake tin. Turn the
mixture into the tin and bake in a
preheated moderate oven, 180°C
(350°F), Gas Mark 4, for 1½ to 1¾
hours. Turn onto a wire rack to cool.

Cut the cake in half and sandwich
together with the jam. Place on a
cake board and brush the top and
sides with the apricot glaze.

Turn the satin icing onto a surface
dusted with icing sugar. Roll out
thinly then lift onto the rolling pin
and place over the top of the cake.
Dip your hands in icing sugar and
press the icing onto the cake by
rubbing the surface with a circular
movement. Work the surplus icing
to the base of the cake and cut off.

Put the royal icing into a greaseproof paper piping bag fitted with a
No. 2 writing nozzle and pipe a line
1 cm (½ inch) in from the edge of
the cake. Pipe dots on each side of
the line. Decorate the top with roses.
Makes one valentine cake

Mothers' Day Daisy Cake

4-egg Victoria
   sandwich cake
   mixture*
125 g (4 oz)
   strawberry jam
4 tablespoons Apricot
   glaze (see page
   14)
500 g (1 lb) Fondant
   icing (see page 25)
125 g (4 oz) pink
   Crème au beurre
   (see page 10)
50 g (2 oz) pink
   Royal icing*
moulded daisies to
   decorate (see page
   28)

Line and grease two 20 cm (8 inch) sandwich tins. Divide the mixture evenly between the tins and bake in a preheated moderate oven, 180°C (350°F), Gas Mark 4, for 25 to 30 minutes. Cool on a wire rack.

Sandwich the cakes together with jam. Place on a wire rack and brush the top and sides with apricot glaze.

Heat the fondant icing gently, stirring, until smooth. Place the wire rack over a plate. Pour the icing over the cake, allowing it to run down the sides and tilting the cake if necessary to help coat it evenly; the icing should not be spread with a knife or the gloss will be spoiled. Leave to set, then trim off any excess icing. Place on a cake board.

Put the crème au beurre into a nylon piping bag fitted with a 5 mm (¼ inch) fluted nozzle and pipe a decorative border around the base of the cake. Put the royal icing in a greaseproof paper piping bag and snip off the end. Write 'Mother' on the cake. Arrange the daisies in clusters around the top edge and pipe a looped edging between the clusters.
Makes one 20 cm (8 inch) cake

Chocolate Celebration Cake

4-egg chocolate
    Whisked sponge
    mixture*
350 g (12 oz)
    chocolate Crème
    au beurre (see
    page 10)
chocolate curls made
    from 175 g (6 oz)
    plain chocolate
    (see page 34)

Grease and flour a 25 cm (10 inch) round cake tin. Turn the mixture into the tin and bake in a preheated moderately hot oven, 190°C (375°F), Gas Mark 5, for 35 to 40 minutes. Turn onto a wire rack to cool.

Cut the cake in half and sandwich together with one third of the icing. Cover the sides with more icing. Coat with chocolate curls. Spread half the remaining icing over the top of the cake, with a palette knife.

Mark a 23 cm (9 inch) circle on a piece of waxed paper. Melt the remaining chocolate. Pour half onto the waxed paper and spread to the edge of the circle. Leave until just set then cut into 16 wedges. Use the remaining chocolate to decorate the triangles (see page 34). Leave to set.

Put the remaining icing into a nylon piping bag fitted with a 5 mm (¼ inch) fluted nozzle and pipe a decorative border around the edge of the cake. Arrange the chocolate triangles on the cake at an angle.

Makes one 25 cm (10 inch) cake

Hallowe'en Pumpkin

*4-egg Victoria
  sandwich cake
  mixture**
*50 g (2 oz) Butter
  icing (see page 11)*
*500 g (1 lb) orange
  Moulding icing
  (see page 27)*
*50 g (2 oz) green
  Moulding icing
  (see page 27)*
TO DECORATE:
liquorice allsorts

Grease and flour two 1.2 litre (2 pint)
ovenproof pudding basins. Divide
the mixture evenly between them
and bake in a preheated moderate
oven, 160°C (325°F), Gas Mark 3, for
1 hour 30 to 45 minutes. Turn onto a
wire rack to cool.

Sandwich the flat side of each cake
together with all except 1 tablespoon
of the butter icing, to make a ball
shape. Cut a shallow hole in the
centre of the top of the cake. Mark 6
lines from the centre of the top and
down the sides of the cake. Cut a
small ridge along each marked line.
Place on a cake board.

Roll out the orange icing thinly to
a 25 cm (10 inch) circle on a surface
dusted with cornflour. Lift it onto
the rolling pin and lay over the cake.
Dip your fingers in cornflour and
smooth the icing over the cake,
pressing it gently into the grooves.

Shape a piece of green icing into
eyebrows and jagged teeth. Use
liquorice allsorts for the eyes and
nose. Secure with butter icing. Shape
green icing into leaves and a stalk.
Place in the centre of the cake.
Makes one hallowe'en cake

Simnel Cake

20 cm (8 inch) round
Rich fruit cake
mixture*
800 g (1¾ lb)
Almond paste*
2 tablespoons Apricot
glaze (see page
14)
1 egg white, beaten

Place half the mixture in a prepared 20 cm (8 inch) round deep cake tin. Roll a quarter of the almond paste to a 20 cm (8 inch) circle. Lay on top of the mixture and press lightly. Spread remaining mixture on top.

Bake in a preheated moderate oven, 160°C (325°F), Gas Mark 3, for 1 hour; lower the temperature to 150°C (300°F), Gas Mark 2, and bake for a further 2½ hours. Leave in the tin for 5 minutes then turn onto a wire rack to cool.

Roll out a third of the remaining almond paste to a 20 cm (8 inch) circle. Brush the top of the cake with apricot glaze, press the paste on top and mark a diamond pattern. Shape remaining paste into balls and place around the edge. Brush with egg white and brown under a hot grill; cool. Tie a ribbon around the cake.
Makes one 20 cm (8 inch) cake

Harvest Cake

350 g (12 oz)
yellow Moulding
icing (see page 27)
1 × 20 cm (8 inch)
square Rich fruit
cake, covered with
almond paste*
1 egg white
125 g (4 oz) deep
yellow Royal
icing*
almond paste fruit
and vegetables (see
page 30-31)

Roll out the moulding icing on a surface dusted with cornflour to a 25 cm (10 inch) square. Brush the almond paste with a little egg white, then lift the icing onto the rolling pin and place over the top of the cake. Dip your hands in cornflour and press the icing onto the sides of the cake by rubbing the surface with a circular movement. Work the surplus to the base and cut off.

Using a No. 2 writing nozzle and a little of the royal icing, pipe 'Harvest' across the top of the cake as shown. Arrange the fruit and vegetables below. Using a 5 mm (¼ inch) fluted nozzle and the remaining icing, pipe a shell border round the bottom edge of the cake.
Makes one harvest cake

ROYAL ICING TECHNIQUES

Royal icing is used for wedding and celebration cakes when a flat surface is required for applying decorations. It sets hard and will keep for a long time. It also protects the cake and keeps it moist. To achieve a really smooth white icing, it is necessary to apply 3 coats. If a peaked effect is required, one coat is sufficient.

Royal icing is also used for piping designs onto flat iced cakes, using a variety of nozzles, and for making flowers, doves and many other applied decorations.

Equipment

As well as the basic equipment already described (see page 6), there are some additional pieces of equipment which you will find helpful when using royal icing. Most of these can be obtained from kitchenware shops, but a wider range is available from cake decorating schools.

An *icing turntable*, though not essential, does give a better result for the sides of the cake.

An *icing ruler* is essential for a smooth finish on the top of a cake. Both plastic and stainless steel ones are available.

An *icing scraper* or *comb* makes smoothing the sides of the cake much easier.

A *greaseproof paper* piping bag is the simplest to use for royal icing. If you are using different nozzles or icing a large cake it's a good idea to make several (see page 7). If you use a nylon piping bag, you will need a collar and connector; insert the connector into the bag and screw the nozzle onto the connector.

A good selection of *piping nozzles* makes icing more fun and provides more scope for design.

A *piping nail* is essential when making piped flowers.

Waxed paper is the best to use for run-outs or piping flowers, though silicone paper can also be used.

A *compass* is useful when making circular designs.

Thick *cake boards* are used for royal iced cakes. The cake should be placed on a board 5 cm (2 inches) larger than the cake; for the bottom tier of a wedding cake the board can be up to 10 cm (4 inches) larger.

COVERING WITH ALMOND PASTE

Almond paste is used to cover rich fruit cakes before covering with royal, moulding or satin icing. It gives a smooth finish on which to work and prevents the icing being discoloured by the moisture from the cake.

After covering the cake with almond paste, leave to dry at room temperature for 2 to 3 days. If a finished cake is going to be stored for a long time, leave the paste to dry for 5 to 7 days before icing is applied.

For quantities and instructions for making almond paste, see pages 89 to 91.

To cover the top of the cake: Sift a little icing sugar onto a work surface. Roll out half the almond paste to a 1 cm (½ inch) thickness and a square or circle 1 cm (½ inch) larger than the top of the cake.

To cover the side of a round cake: Brush with apricot glaze. Cut a piece of string the circumference of the cake and another piece of string the exact depth of the cake.

Brush the top of the cake with apricot glaze (see page 14) and place the cake upside down on the paste. Using a small palette knife, draw up the edge of the paste level to the side of the cake. Smooth evenly all round, trimming away any surplus paste.

To cover the sides of a square cake: Roll out the remaining paste and cut 4 rectangles to fit each side of the cake. Press them gently onto the cake and smooth the joins together with a small palette knife. Place on a cake board.

Roll out the remaining paste to a strip to fit exactly round the cake, using the pieces of string as your guide. Trim and roll up like a Swiss roll.

Unroll the strip carefully around the cake. Press ends together with a small palette knife. Place on a cake board.

COVERING WITH ROYAL ICING

For quantities and instructions for making royal icing, see pages 89 to 91. Secure the cake to the board with a little icing, before starting.

To ice the top of the cake: Spoon some icing onto the top of the cake and spread it over the surface with a palette knife, using a paddling movement.

Draw an icing ruler across the top of the cake towards you, holding the ruler at a slight angle. Remove surplus icing with a knife held parallel with the side of the cake. Leave to dry.

To ice the side of a round cake: Place the cake on a turntable or upturned plate. Spread some icing onto the side of the cake, using a small palette knife to make it as smooth as possible.
Hold an icing scraper at a 45° angle to the cake and with the other hand, rotate the turntable so that the side is smoothed in one movement. Remove surplus icing from the top and base with a palette knife. Leave to dry.

To ice the sides of a square cake: Ice 2 opposite sides using a small palette knife. Leave to set then ice the other 2 sides. Take care to remove surplus icing from the top edge and corners to form sharp edges.

For a smooth finish: When completely dry, remove any rough edges from the icing using a sharp knife, then fine sandpaper and a clean brush.

Apply 2 more coats of thin icing in the same way, making sure each coat is completely dry before adding the next. Leave to dry before decorating.

To ice the board, spread a thin layer of icing around the cake with a small palette knife. Hold the knife at an angle and smooth in one movement by turning the turntable with the other hand. Remove surplus icing on the edge.

45

PIPED DESIGNS

Most piped designs can be made using plain (writing) or star nozzles. Before embarking on a royal iced cake, practise piping lines, loops, rosettes, etc, onto a work surface.

Royal icing for piping must be free from lumps and air bubbles. During piping, keep the bowl of icing covered with a damp cloth or plastic cling film to prevent drying.

Using a plain nozzle

A variety of designs can be achieved using simple plain nozzles. They are available in a range of sizes: No. 00 to 4. For most purposes, only a No. 1 and 2 writing nozzle are required; unless otherwise stated, use either of these nozzles, depending on the degree of fineness required.

Straight lines

Squeeze out enough icing to touch the surface then, squeezing the bag gently, lift the nozzle a little above the surface and pull it gently towards you. The icing should come out in a slightly sagging line, which can be manoeuvred to keep straight. To finish, simply touch the surface with the nozzle.

Loops

Hold the nozzle away from the cake and move to allow the icing to fall in an even loop. If the cake is tilted, the finished loop will rest more easily.

Trellis

Pipe a series of parallel straight lines over the area to be covered, using a No. 1 or 2 writing nozzle. When dry, turn the cake and pipe another layer of parallel lines over the first layer, to give a diamond effect. For a more delicate effect, using a No. 1 writing nozzle, pipe a third and fourth layer over the top, allowing each layer to dry first.

Writing

Using a No. 1 or 2 nozzle, practise piping simple capital letters, then progress to hand writing. Draw the words on greaseproof paper and prick them onto the surface of the iced cake with a pin. This ensures that the words are positioned correctly. A second layer of icing piped with a finer tube, perhaps using a different coloured icing, is most effective.

Rope design

Move the piping bag in a circular movement making a series of 'e' shaped twists. This is useful for neatening trellis.

Dots

These make simple, attractive borders. Use No. 1 to 4 nozzles.

Picot edge

An easy decoration combining curved lines and dots. It is very useful as a top edge on the side of a cake.

Lacework

Hold the nozzle close to the cake and pipe a continuous wiggly line, keeping the spaces an even size.

MERRY CHRISTMAS

Happy Birthday

Using a star nozzle

A star nozzle can be used to create all of the designs described below. Star nozzles vary in the size of the top of the nozzle and in the number of points. The smaller No. 42, 43 and 44 star nozzles are most useful for royal icing.

Star

Hold the piping bag upright just above the surface of the cake. Squeeze the icing from the bag, then make a quick down and up movement to give a squat star.

Rosette

Hold the piping bag upright just above the surface of the cake. Squeeze the icing out in a circular movement towards the centre. Curl it into the centre and finish off sharply, leaving a slightly raised point in the middle.

Shell

Using a star or shell nozzle, hold the piping bag just above the surface of the cake and at an angle to it. Squeeze the icing out onto the cake until a head is formed. Pull the bag gently back and at the same time release the pressure. The shell should come to a neat point. Repeat to form a border.

Scroll

Using a star or shell nozzle, hold the piping bag just above the surface of the cake at an angle. Squeeze out the icing into a large comma shape, beginning with a thick head and gradually releasing pressure on the bag while pulling into a long tail. Repeat all around the cake. When dry, a second smaller scroll may be piped on top using a smaller shell or star nozzle, or a plain writing nozzle.

PIPED DECORATIONS

Miniature bell

Using a No. 4 writing nozzle, pipe a large dot onto waxed paper, a smaller dot on top, then a third even smaller one in one movement. Leave to dry for several hours until the outside is firm and the inside still soft.

Remove the paper and scoop out the soft icing in the centre to make a thin shell. Secure a silver ball in each bell with a little icing.

Dove

Using a No. 4 writing nozzle, pipe the body onto waxed paper, pressing the icing out into a bulb shape. Raise the bag a little to form the neck and press again to form the head. Pull off quickly to make the beak.

Using a No. 1 nozzle, pipe the wings and tail onto waxed paper. Allow to dry.

When the icing is firm carefully remove the paper. Assemble the sections, securing them with a little icing. Paint in 2 eyes with black food colouring and paint the beak with yellow colouring.

PIPED FLOWERS

To pipe flowers you need a large, medium or fine petal nozzle, depending on the size of flower required; an icing nail; and small squares of waxed paper. Place a little icing on top of the nail and stick a square of waxed paper on top. Leave flowers to dry for 24 hours before removing paper.

Rose

Hold the piping bag with the thin part of the nozzle up. Pipe a cone of icing, twisting the nail quickly between finger and thumb.

Pipe 3 to 5 overlapping petals around the centre of the rose, allowing the outer petals to curve outwards.

Apple Blossom

Working with the thick edge of the nozzle to the centre and keeping it flat, pipe 5 small rounded white petals.

Pipe a yellow dot in the centre. Paint the edges with pink food colouring.

Primrose

Use yellow icing and work with the thick edge of the nozzle to the centre, keeping it flat. Pipe from the centre outwards. Go halfway back in, then out again, then back to the centre to give a heart-shaped petal.

Pipe 5 petals in all. Using a No. 1 writing nozzle, pipe a dot in the middle.

Narcissus

Use yellow icing and work with the thick edge of the nozzle to the centre, keeping it flat. Pipe a petal, then make 5 more petals, starting just under the previous one each time. Leave to dry.

Using a small petal nozzle pipe the centre, twisting the nail quickly to make a complete circle. Paint the edges of the trumpet and petals with yellow food colouring.

Forget-me-nots

These are best piped straight onto the cake. Using a No. 2 writing nozzle and blue icing, pipe 5 or 6 dots touching each other in a circle. Pipe a yellow dot in the centre of each. Pipe curved green lines as stalks.

Leaves

Large leaves may be piped with a leaf nozzle.

A piping bag without a nozzle gives a better effect for smaller leaves. Fill the greaseproof paper bag but don't cut off the tip. Press the tip of the bag flat, then snip off the point in the shape of an arrow. Place the tip of the bag on the paper, holding it at a slight angle. Press out the icing and pull away quickly to make a tapering point. Mark on a vein with a cocktail stick.

Serrated fern-like leaves can be made by moving the tube back and forwards.

When practised, leaves may be piped straight onto the cake.

RUN-OUTS

A run-out is a shaped piece of icing, such as an initial, number, flower, leaf, animal or figure. They can be used for Christmas cake decorations too: Father Christmas, snowmen, robins, Christmas trees, stars, etc.

For a simple run-out shape, pipe the outline straight onto the cake and then flood with icing (see below).

For more difficult shapes, it is easier to pipe the outline onto a piece of waxed paper and then flood with icing. Outlines for Father Christmas, robins and other motifs can be traced from the stencils on pages 92-93. Alternatively, outlines can be traced from designs on Christmas cards.

Run-outs can be stored in an airtight container for a few months without discolouring.

Preparing the shape

Draw or trace the outline onto a piece of card. Secure a piece of waxed paper over the card. Using a No. 2 writing nozzle and icing the same colour as that to be used for flooding, trace the outline of the drawing. Move the waxed paper along over the card to make the required number of shapes; always make more than you need to allow for breakages when removing paper.

Flooding the shape

Thin down a little royal icing with egg white until it is a flowing consistency. Spoon it into the centre of the outline, making a slight dome; if it is a very small area pipe in the icing using a No. 3 writing nozzle. Use a cocktail stick to ease the icing into corners, and to prick any air bubbles. Leave to dry, then pipe in lines or dots to complete the detail of the run-out or paint with food colouring.

Removing the paper

Leave for 2 to 3 days to dry completely then remove the paper: place the run-out on a thick book, slightly overlapping the edge. Pull the paper gently downwards, then turn the run-out round, pulling the paper away until all the edges are loose. Gently pull off the paper. Secure the run-out in position on the cake with a little royal icing.

Butterfly

Outline the wings and body separately. Carefully flood each section with icing and leave to dry.

Pipe 2 antennae with a No. 1 writing nozzle. Decorate the wings with piped lines and dots, using a No. 1 writing nozzle, or paint on with food colouring. Use a little icing to attach the wings and antennae to the body at a slight angle. Hold the wings in position with small pieces of plasticine until dry.

Flowers

Outline the flower. Flood each petal using a No. 3 writing nozzle and leave to dry.

Pipe an outline around each petal and several dots in the centre with a No. 1 writing nozzle. Diluted food colouring may be used to paint the petals, using dark shades in the centre and pale towards the outer edges.

Run-out pansies are extremely pretty, especially when two shades are used in the same flower. Outline the large lower petal in each flower, flood with icing and leave to dry. When set, outline the remaining petals and fill with a lighter shade. To finish, paint streaks from the centre of the petals with food colouring.

Ivy leaves

Outline the leaf, then flood. When dry, use a No. 1 writing nozzle and pipe a thin line of icing down the centre to make a vein and stalk.

DESIGNING THE CAKE

Most designs on cakes are regular geometric shapes because they ensure the cake will look good from every angle. Once you have mastered the basic techniques, you can create your own designs, getting ideas from cakes in confectioners' windows, wallpapers, pieces of lace, and other sources.

Loops make a very attractive decoration around the sides of a cake. They can be piped simply or elaborated with dots, made with fine, medium and thick writing nozzles, and flowers used singly or in clusters of 3.

Most designs need to be carefully drawn to scale and a template made for accurate marking on the cake.

Making a simple template
For the top: Cut a piece of greaseproof paper the size of the top of the cake. Fold in half 3 times to make a cone shape; crease the edges well. Draw the scallop or desired shape on the paper, using a compass, base of a glass or other suitable object. Prick along the line with a pin right through paper. Open out and secure on top of the cake with pins. Use a pin to prick along the outline of the design. Remove paper and the design will be marked on the cake.
For the sides: Measure the depth of the cake and cut a band of greaseproof paper to size. Fold it to give the required size and number of scallops, etc. Draw the design on the paper and open out. Secure on top of the cake and mark design with pins as above.

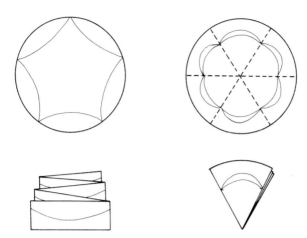

Silver Wedding Cake Templates (recipe, page 61)
For the top: Cut out a 25 cm (10 inch) circle of grease-proof paper and mark 5 equally spaced points on the circumference.

Using a compass or the base of a suitable-sized glass, draw 5 scallops, joining the marks on the paper and making them about 5 cm (2 inches) deep on the curve. Position the template and mark the design as described.

For the side: Measure and cut a band of greaseproof paper as described. Place it around the cake and secure with pins. Mark the points of the scallops already marked on the top of the cake. Remove the paper and draw in the scallops as for the top, but not quite so deep. Secure the band to the cake with pins, placing it a little above centre so that the points of top and side curves almost meet. Mark the design as described.

Rose Wedding Cake Templates (recipe, page 64)
For the top: Cut out and fold 3 greaseproof paper circles as described. Open out and place on the cakes. Using a compass or the base of a suitable sized glass, mark an outward facing scallop between each crease; make the curve about 5 cm (2 inches) in from the side of the larger cake, 2.5 cm (1 inch) in for the middle tier and 1 cm (½ inch) in for the top tier. Remove the paper from the cakes and draw in the design firmly. Position the template and mark the design as described.

For the side: Measure and cut 3 bands of greaseproof paper as described. Fold each into 6 sections. Draw a scallop as described for the top, to correspond with the one on the top of each cake but not quite so deep. Place around the cake, matching the curves on the top. Position the template and mark the design as described.

Christmas Bell Cake

23 cm (9 inch)
  square Rich fruit
  cake, covered with
  almond paste*
900 g (2 lb) white
  Royal icing*
red food colouring
18-20 sugar bells
  (see below)

Cover the cake with 3 layers of royal icing, allowing it to dry between each coat, then ice the board.

Fit a greaseproof paper piping bag with a No. 43 star nozzle and half fill with royal icing. Pipe a row of shells around the top and bottom edges of the cake. Using a No. 44 star nozzle pipe another row of shells around the edge of the board. Colour a little icing red. Fit a greaseproof paper piping bag with a No. 2 writing nozzle and half fill with the red icing. Pipe a line of icing all round the top of the cake inside the shell border. Pipe 2 lines of red icing on the board around the cake.

Arrange a cluster of 3 bells at each corner of the cake on the board. Arrange the remaining bells in a cluster in one top corner of the cake. Write 'Nöel' in the opposite corner. Outline the inner edge of the other corners with 2 right-angled red lines to complete the design. Tie a red ribbon around the cake.

Makes one 23 cm (9 inch) cake

Sugar Bells: Place 2 tablespoons granulated sugar in a basin and gradually mix in a few drops of egg white until the mixture is crumbly. Press into a bell mould, then tip out. Repeat to make 20 bells. Leave to dry.

When the bells are firm to the touch on the outside, but still soft in the centre, scoop out the centres to make the bells as fine as possible.

Pipe a little white royal icing into each bell, using a greaseproof paper piping bag fitted with a No. 1 writing nozzle and press in silver balls.

Sugar bells are fragile and must be handled carefully. Make more than the number required to allow for breakage.

Snow Scene Christmas Cake

20 cm (8 inch) round
    Rich fruit cake,
    covered with
    almond paste*
675 g (1½ lb) white
    Royal icing*
1 moulded Father
    Christmas (see
    page 32)
5 moulded fir trees
    (see page 32)

Cover the cake completely with the royal icing until evenly coated. Using the tip of a small palette knife, press the surface of the icing and draw it away again sharply to make a peak. Repeat all over the cake.

Place the Father Christmas and fir trees on top of the cake.

Makes one 20 cm (8 inch) cake

Holly Leaf Christmas Cake

23 cm (9 inch) round
    Rich fruit cake,
    covered with
    almond paste*
675 g (1½ lb) white
    Royal icing*
125 g (4 oz) red
    Royal icing*
12 almond paste
    holly leaves and
    36 berries (see
    page 32)

Cover the cake with 3 layers of white royal icing, allowing the icing to dry between each coat, then ice the board.

Fit a greaseproof paper piping bag with a No. 44 star nozzle and half fill with white royal icing. Pipe a row of shells around the top and bottom edges of the cake.

Fit a greaseproof paper piping bag with a No. 1 writing nozzle and half-fill with red royal icing. Pipe a red line around the top of the cake and pipe a line of red dots inside.

Fit another greaseproof paper piping bag with a No. 2 writing nozzle and half fill with white icing. Write 'Happy Christmas' on top of the cake. When dry, overpipe with red icing. Position 2 holly leaves and a cluster of 3 berries below 'Happy Christmas'.

Arrange the remaining leaves and berries all around the side of the cake, securing with a little icing. Pipe a picot design on either side of the leaves near the shell borders, using the white icing for the looped border and red icing for the dots.

Makes one 23 cm (9 inch) cake

Golden Wedding Anniversary Cake

23 cm (9 inch)
    square Rich fruit
    cake, covered with
    almond paste*
675 g (1½ lb) white
    Royal icing*
125 g (4 oz) yellow
    Royal icing
yellow moulded roses
    (see page 28)

Cover the cake with 3 layers of white royal icing, allowing it to dry between each coat; ice the board.

Fit a greaseproof paper piping bag with a No. 3 writing nozzle; half fill with white icing. Pipe dot borders around the top and bottom edges of the cake and along the board.

Fit a greaseproof paper piping bag with a No. 2 writing nozzle and half fill with white icing. Fit another bag with a No. 2 writing nozzle and half fill with yellow icing. Pipe a picot edge along the sides of the cake, using white icing for the looped border and yellow for the dots. Pipe 2 yellow lines around the board.

Arrange the roses in one corner of the cake, securing with a little icing. Using white icing and a No. 2 nozzle, pipe '50' in the opposite corner. When dry, overpipe with yellow icing. Outline the inner edge of the other corners with 2 yellow lines. Tie a ribbon round the cake.

Makes one 23 cm (9 inch) cake

Silver Wedding Anniversary Cake

25 cm (10 inch)
  round Rich fruit
  cake, covered with
  almond paste*
1.25 kg (2½ lb)
  white Royal
  icing*
30 white piped roses
  (see page 50)

Cover the cake with 3 layers of royal icing, allowing it to dry between each coat, then ice the board.

Make a template (see page 55) and mark the design on the cake.

Fit a greaseproof paper piping bag with a No. 2 writing nozzle, half fill with icing and outline the design, covering the pin pricks completely. Using a No. 1 writing nozzle, fill in the scallops with lacework and pipe lacework·on the board.

Pipe '25' in the centre of the cake using a No. 2 writing nozzle. Using a No. 3 writing nozzle, pipe dots around the base of the cake.

Fix the flowers in clusters of 3 between the scallops on the top and side of the cake, with a little icing.

Using a No. 1 writing nozzle, overpipe the 25 on top of the cake. Pipe a loop under each scallop on the side of the cake.

Makes one 25 cm (10 inch) cake

Christening Cake

25 cm (10 inch)
   square Rich fruit
   cake, covered with
   almond paste*
900 g (2 lb) pale
   pink or blue Royal
   icing*
500 g (1 lb) white
   Royal icing*
4 piped doves and 36
   bells (see page
   49)

Cover the cake with 3 layers of pink or blue icing, allowing to dry between each coat, then ice the board.

Using a No. 2 writing nozzle and white icing, pipe a trellis all round the top of the cake, starting 2.5 cm (1 inch) in from the top edge and finishing 1 cm (½ inch) down the side of the cake. Repeat round the bottom and down each corner.

When dry, pipe another trellis on top, using a No. 1 writing nozzle. Allow to dry. Using a No. 1 writing nozzle, join the edges of the trellis on the sides and board with loops.

Using a No. 2 writing nozzle and white icing, pipe 2 curved lines on top of the cake, joining the corners. Finish with a line of dots. Pipe a similar curved design on the sides.

Arrange a dove in each corner and the bells in clusters of 3 around the sides, fixing them with a little icing. Pipe a line of dots below each cluster.

Write the baby's name on the cake in white, using a No. 2 nozzle. Leave to dry, then overpipe with pink or blue icing, using a No. 1 nozzle.

Makes one 25 cm (10 inch) cake

21st Birthday Cake

23 cm (9 inch) round
  Rich fruit cake,
  covered with
  almond paste*
900 g (2 lb) white
  Royal icing*
blue or pink food
  colourings

Cover the cake with 3 layers of royal icing, allowing to dry between each coat, then ice the board. Make a simple top scallop template (see page 54); mark the design on the cake.

Using a No. 2 writing nozzle, outline the design, covering the pin marks completely. Pipe a trellis in each scallop and leave to dry. Colour a little icing blue or pink and pipe over the trellis, using a No. 1 nozzle.

Using a No. 44 star nozzle, pipe a star border around the bottom edge of the cake. Using a No. 42 star nozzle, pipe similar borders around the top of the cake and along the edge of the board.

Pipe evenly spaced white forget-me-nots (see page 51) around the side of the cake and board. Join the flowers with stalks, making a curved design. Pipe a few leaves on the stalks. When dry, overpipe the flowers with blue or pink icing.

Pipe '21' on the cake using white icing and a No. 2 writing nozzle. When dry, overpipe with blue or pink icing, using a No. 1 nozzle.

Makes one 23 cm (9 inch) cake

WEDDING CAKES

When making a wedding cake, it is most important to choose the sizes of the tiers carefully. For a 3-tier cake a good proportion would be 15, 23 and 30 cm (6, 9 and 12 inches). For a 2-tier cake 20 and 30 cm (8 and 12 inches), or 18 and 25 cm (7 and 10 inches), or 15 and 23 cm (6 and 9 inches) would all be suitable.

The tiers should also vary in height, the bottom one being about 7.5 cm (3 inches) high, the middle one 6 cm (2½ inches) and the top tier 5 cm (2 inches) high.

When royal icing a tiered wedding cake, omit the glycerine in the royal icing for all tiers except the top one, otherwise the icing will not be firm enough to support the weight of the cakes.

Cake boards should be 5 cm (2 inches) larger than the cakes so they project 2.5 cm (1 inch) all round when the cake is covered with marzipan and icing. The bottom tier looks better on a board 7.5 to 10 cm (3 to 4 inches) larger than the cake.

3-Tier Rose Wedding Cake

1 each 15, 20 and
25 cm (6, 8 and
10 inch) round
Rich fruit cakes,
covered with
almond paste*
2.25 kg (5 lb) white
Royal icing*
36 piped white roses
and 72 leaves (see
page 50)

Cover the cakes with 3 layers of royal icing, allowing it to dry between each coat, then ice the boards.

Make the templates (see page 55) and mark the design on the cakes.

Fit a greaseproof paper piping bag with a No. 2 writing nozzle, half fill with icing and outline the designs, covering the pin pricks completely. Pipe a second line inside the scallop on the top of each cake, and below the scallop on the side. Place a rose and 2 leaves at the point of each scallop, securing with a little icing. Using the same nozzle, pipe dots below each rose on the side.

Fit a greaseproof paper piping bag with a No. 44 star nozzle. Pipe a shell border around the top and bottom edges of each cake.

Assemble the cakes, using 8 white pillars, and place a fresh flower arrangement on top of the cake.
Makes one 3-tier round cake

2-Tier Butterfly Wedding Cake

1 each 18 and 25 cm (7 and 10 inch) square Rich fruit cakes, covered with almond paste*
2 kg (4 lb) white Royal icing*
250 g (8 oz) yellow Royal icing*
12 white butterfly run-outs (see page 53)

Cover the cakes with 3 layers of royal icing, allowing it to dry between each coat, then ice the boards.

Mark the centre point of each side on the top of the cakes. Join by marking a line with a pin to make a diamond shape.

Fit a greaseproof paper piping bag with a No. 2 writing nozzle, half fill with white icing and pipe a line to cover the pin marks. Pipe a trellis in the 4 corners of the cakes. Leave to dry, then using a No. 1 nozzle and yellow icing, cover with a second layer of trellis work. Neaten the edges of the trellis with a row of stars using a No. 42 star nozzle.

Using a No. 44 star nozzle, pipe a star border at the bottom edge of the cakes. Using a No. 42 star nozzle, pipe a star border around the edges of the boards.

Using a No. 2 writing nozzle, pipe 3 looped lines on each side of the cakes, making 2 loops on each side. Pipe a series of dots from the points where the loops meet.

Using the same nozzle, pipe 3 parallel lines on the bottom board and 2 lines on the top one. Overpipe these lines and the dots with yellow icing, using a No. 1 nozzle.

Using the yellow icing and a No. 1 writing nozzle, outline the butterflies and pipe dots around the wings. Leave to dry. Place a butterfly at each corner of the boards. Arrange butterflies at the points of the diamonds on the larger cake.

Assemble the cakes using 4 white pillars and place a fresh flower arrangement on the top of the cake.
Makes one 2-tier square cake

NOVELTY CAKES

It is difficult at a children's party to focus attention on the birthday cake when there are so many other goodies on the table. One way of overcoming this is to produce a novelty cake; it can be a simple round sponge, decorated as a clock, drum or maypole, but still effective. Or it can be a more unusual and exciting cake.

If you choose a design that requires cutting to shape, make the cake the day before so that it is not too crumbly; a Victoria sandwich cake is the easiest to cut. To avoid the crumbs getting mixed in with the icing and spoiling the finished effect, brush the cake with apricot glaze first.

The decorations can almost always be sweets but a little simple piping is sometimes needed to give the best result.

Large cake boards are useful as bases for the cakes, though a chopping board covered in foil makes a good substitute. Alternatively novelty cakes may be placed on thin cake cards onto which they fit exactly.

Ladybird

4-egg chocolate
   Victoria sandwich
   cake mixture*
125 g (4 oz) Apricot
   glaze (see page 14)
500 g (1 lb) red
   Moulding icing
   (see note and
   recipe on page 27)
liquorice ribbon
black food colouring
small round liquorice
   sweets
few smarties
125 g (4 oz) green
   desiccated coconut
   (see page 14)
piped Royal icing
   flowers (see page
   50)

Grease and flour a 4 litre (7 pint) ovenproof mixing bowl.

Turn the mixture into the bowl and spread evenly to the edges. Bake in a preheated moderate oven, 180°C (350°F), Gas Mark 4, for 1½ to 1¾ hours. Turn onto a wire rack to cool.

Place the cake upside down on a board and brush with the apricot glaze. Roll out the moulding icing thinly on a surface sprinkled with cornflour. Lift the icing on the rolling pin and place on top of the cake. Dip your hands in cornflour and mould the icing to the cake by rubbing the surface with a circular movement. Work the surplus icing to the base of the cake and cut off.

Using the back of a knife, mark a line down the centre of the cake, and a semi-circle at one end to represent a face. Press pieces of liquorice ribbon into the indentations. Paint the face area with black food colouring and leave to dry.

Cut the liquorice sweets into thin rounds and press onto the ladybird. Stick on smarties to represent eyes and mouth, using a little icing. Paint dots on the eyes with black food colouring.

Sprinkle the coconut around the ladybird to represent grass. Scatter a few piped flowers on the grass.

Makes one 'ladybird'

NOTE: For a bright red ladybird, colour the moulding icing with edible red paste colouring. Both this and black food colouring are available from specialist suppliers (see page 95).

Wigwam

3-egg chocolate
  Victoria sandwich
  cake mixture*
4 tablespoons Apricot
  glaze (see page 14)
175 g (6 oz)
  Almond paste*
few strips liquorice
  ribbon
125 g (4 oz) Royal
  icing*
red, blue and yellow
  food colourings
3 almond paste fir
  trees, optional (see
  page 32)

Grease and flour a 1.2 litre (2 pint) ovenproof pudding basin and a ramekin dish. Use the cake mixture to three-quarters fill the basin, ramekin and a fairy cake paper case.

Bake in a preheated moderate oven, 180°C (350°F), Gas Mark 4, allowing 20 minutes for the fairy cake, 35 minutes for the ramekin and 1¼ to 1½ hours for the large cake. Turn onto a wire rack to cool.

Place the cakes on top of each other to form a dome shape, sandwiching them together with a little of the apricot glaze. Shape the cake into a 5-sided pyramid by cutting away 5 equal triangular pieces (see diagram 1). Discard the cut out pieces. Place the cake on a board and brush with apricot glaze.

Roll out the almond paste thinly on a surface lightly dusted with icing sugar to a 30 × 18 cm (12 × 7 inch) rectangle. Cut out 5 equal triangles, 18 cm (7 inches) high and 10 cm (4 inches) across the base (see diagram 2).

Press onto the triangular facets of the cake. Press the sides of the almond paste triangles together but roll back the inside bottom corner of one triangle to form an entrance flap.

Press the liquorice strips into the top of the wigwam to represent poles.

Divide the royal icing into 3 portions; colour one portion red, one green and one yellow. Using greaseproof paper piping bags fitted with No. 2 writing nozzles, pipe a line and dot design on each almond paste triangle as shown.

Place a toy indian at the entrance. Position the trees, if using, in front of the cake, with another toy indian.
Makes one 'wigwam'

diagram 1

diagram 2

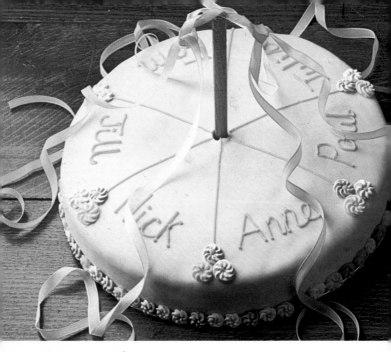

Maypole

4-egg Victoria
  sandwich cake
  mixture*
175 g (6 oz) yellow
  Butter icing (see
  page 11)
2 tablespoons Apricot
  glaze (see page
  14)
500 g (1 lb) yellow
  Moulding icing
  (see page 27)
125 g (4 oz) deep,
  yellow Glacé icing
  (see page 11)
1 stick barley sugar
sugar flowers

Line and grease a 25 cm (10 inch)
round cake tin. Turn the mixture
into the tin and bake in a preheated
moderate oven, 180°C (350°F), Gas
Mark 4, for 35 to 40 minutes. Turn
onto a wire rack to cool.

Split the cake in half and sandwich
together with the butter icing. Brush
the cake with the apricot glaze. Roll
out the moulding icing thinly on a
board dusted with cornflour to a
33 cm (13 inch) circle and use to
cover the cake, see Ladybird
(page 69).

Put the glacé icing into a
greaseproof paper piping bag fitted
with a No. 2 writing nozzle. Pipe 6
lines from the centre of the cake to
the edge. Write a name in each
triangle.

Attach ribbons to one end of the
barley sugar. Press into the centre of
the cake, allowing one ribbon to fall
to each name. Decorate with sugar
flowers.

Makes one 'maypole'

Clock Cake

4-egg Victoria
  sandwich cake
  mixture*
175 g (6 oz)
  chocolate Butter
  icing (see page 11)
2 × 100 g (3½ oz)
  packets milk
  chocolate finger
  biscuits
250 g (8 oz) Glacé
  icing (see page 9)
1 teaspoon cocoa
  powder

Line and grease two 20 cm (8 inch)
sandwich tins. Turn the mixture into
the tins and bake in a preheated
moderate oven, 180°C (350°F), Gas
Mark 4, for 30 to 35 minutes. Turn
onto a wire rack to cool.

Sandwich the cakes together with
three quarters of the butter icing.
Cover the sides with the remaining
butter icing and place on a board.
Trim the chocolate fingers to the
height of the cake and arrange
around the edge.

Spread three quarters of the glacé
icing over the top of the cake and
leave to set. Add the cocoa to the
remaining glacé icing and put into a
greaseproof paper piping bag fitted
with a No. 2 writing nozzle.

Pipe a circle of dots around the top
of the cake. Pipe on the clock
numbers and the hands, pointing to
the o'clock corresponding with the
child's age.

Makes one 'clock'

Fairy Castle

6-egg Victoria
  sandwich cake
  mixture*
1 packet lemon jelly
blue food colouring
350 g (12 oz) Butter
  icing (see page 11)
3 tablespoons Apricot
  glaze (see page 14)
4 round ice cream
  cones
2 miniature Swiss
  rolls
2 large Swiss rolls
½ wagon wheel
sugar strands
175 g (6 oz) white
  Glacé icing (see
  page 9)
2 ice cream wafers
125 g (4 oz) bar
  nougat, cut into
  small rectangles
sugar flowers
50 g (2 oz) green
  Glacé icing (see
  page 9)

Line and grease two deep 20 cm
(8 inch) square cake tins. Divide the
mixture between them. Bake in a
preheated moderate oven, 180°C
(350°F), Gas Mark 4, for 1 to 1¼
hours. Cool on a wire rack.

Make up the jelly, adding blue
colouring while it is still liquid.

Cut a 5 cm (2 inch) slice from one
cake and cut steps (see diagram 1).
Stick onto one side of the larger cake
with butter icing. Sandwich the cakes
together with butter icing as shown
in diagram 2. Trim a 2.5 cm (1 inch)
triangular section from each rear
corner. Brush cake with apricot glaze.

Trim 2.5 cm (1 inch) from the top
of 2 ice cream cones; discard. Cover
the miniature Swiss rolls, the 4 cones
and sides of the cake with butter icing.

Colour three quarters of the
remaining butter icing blue. Use to
cover the large Swiss rolls and
wagon wheel. Place the rolls at the
rear corners of the cake and the
wagon wheel at the front.

Place the small rolls at the front
corners and top with the small cones.
Place the larger cones on the rear
Swiss rolls. Cover the front, back,
platform and steps with blue icing.
Sprinkle sugar strands over the steps.

Pour the white glacé icing on top
of the cake and spread to the edges.
Shape the wafers to make doors and
windows; press into position.
Arrange the nougat pieces to
represent battlements. Decorate the
walls with sugar flowers. Pipe on
stalks, using the green glacé icing.

Pipe borders around the spires and
door with the remaining white
butter icing. Chop the jelly and
arrange around the castle as a moat.

Makes one 'fairy castle'

diagram 1

diagram 2

Kitten

4-egg chocolate
    Victoria sandwich
    cake mixture*
350 g (12 oz)
    chocolate Butter
    icing (see page 11)
3 sponge fingers
2 ice cream cones
few liquorice sweets
1 piece red liquorice
    ribbon
few short pieces
    spaghetti

Grease and line a 600 ml (1 pint) and a 1.2 litre (2 pint) ovenproof pudding basin and two-thirds fill each basin with the mixture. Bake in a preheated moderate oven, 180°C (350°F), Gas Mark 4, for 1 hour for the small cake and 1¼ to 1½ hours for the large one. Turn onto a wire rack to cool.

Trim the small cake into a ball for the head. Trim a slice from one side of the large cake to flatten the chest. Place the large cake on a cake board and fix the small one on top with a little butter icing. Position a sponge finger at the side for a tail.

Cut a 1 cm (½ inch) slice off the other sponge fingers. Place them either side of the chest, as legs; position the slices as paws. Cut the tips off the ice cream cones and place on either side of the head for ears.

Cover the kitten with the icing. Shape the sweets for the eyes and nose; press into position. Tie the liquorice round the neck in a bow and position the spaghetti as whiskers.
Makes one 'kitten'

Igloo

2-egg Victoria
   sandwich cake
   mixture*
1 individual Swiss
   roll
125 g (4 oz) Apricot
   glaze (see page
   14)
500 g (1 lb)
   Moulding icing
   (see page 27)
175 g (6 oz) Royal
   icing*
blue food colouring

Grease and flour a 900 ml (1½ pint) ovenproof pudding basin. Turn the mixture into the basin and bake in a preheated moderate oven, 180°C (350°F), Gas Mark 4, for 1¼ to 1½ hours. Turn onto a wire rack to cool, then place flat side down on a board.

Brush the cake and Swiss roll with apricot glaze. Roll out the icing thinly on a surface dusted with cornflour to a 23 cm (9 inch) circle and use to cover cake, see Ladybird (page 69). Roll out the surplus icing and use to cover the Swiss roll. Place in front of the cake, pressing the icing together to join. Using the back of a knife, mark lines over the igloo to represent blocks of snow.

Colour quarter of the royal icing blue, and with a No. 2 writing nozzle, pipe on a chimney hole, outline the entrance and pipe on the child's name.

Cover board with remaining royal icing and lift into peaks with a palette knife to resemble snow.

Makes one 'igloo'

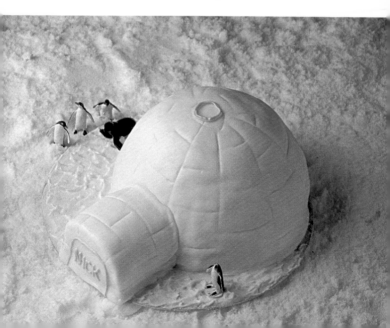

Pram

2-egg Victoria
    sandwich cake
    mixture*
175 g (6 oz) pink
    Butter icing (see
    page 11)
125 g (4 oz)
    Moulding icing
    (see page 27)
1/2 individual Swiss
    roll (halved
    lengthwise)
1 gingerbread man
125 g (4 oz) Royal
    icing*
food colourings
4 round sweet
    biscuits
4 smarties
sugar flowers
liquorice ribbon

Line and grease a 20 cm (8 inch) sandwich tin. Turn the mixture into the tin and bake in a preheated moderate oven, 180°C (350°F), Gas Mark 4, for 30 to 35 minutes. Turn onto a wire rack to cool.

Cut the cake in half to make two semi-circles and sandwich together with some of the butter icing. Cut off and discard a small slice from the rounded end and place the cake, this side down, on a board. Cover the sides with the remaining butter icing.

Roll out the moulding icing thinly on a surface sprinkled with cornflour. Cut out a 15 × 10 cm (6 × 4 inch) rectangle for the blanket. Cut two 10 × 2.5 cm (4 × 1 inch) strips for the under and over sheets. Cover the Swiss roll half with the remaining moulding icing to make a pillow. Place the pillow at the top of the pram and the undersheet next to it.

Cut off and discard the legs of the gingerbread man. Colour a third of the royal icing pink. Colour further portions different colours and pipe a face and jacket on the 'baby'. Lay against the pillow and cover with the blanket. Place the oversheet on top.

Using pink royal icing and a No. 2 writing nozzle, pipe lines onto the biscuits to represent wheels and place a smartie in the centre of each one. Press the wheels into position.

Outline the pillow, top sheet and sides of the pram with pink lines. Then pipe the child's name on the blanket. Using white royal icing and a fluted nozzle, pipe a star border around the edges of the pram, then with a No. 1 writing nozzle, pipe a lacework design on the blanket.

Decorate the sides with sugar flowers. Use the liquorice as a handle.
Makes one 'pram'

diagram 1

diagram 2

Helter Skelter

4-egg Victoria
    sandwich cake
    mixture*
350 g (12 oz)
    chocolate Butter
    icing (see page 11)
12 ice cream wafers
1 round ice cream
    cone
125 g (4 oz) green
    desiccated coconut
    (see page 14)
50 g (2 oz) red
    Butter icing (see
    page 11)
smarties
few jelly babies

Grease and flour a 600 ml (1 pint)
and a 1.2 litre (2 pint) ovenproof
pudding basin. Divide the mixture
between them. Bake in a preheated
moderate oven, 180°C (350°F), Gas
Mark 4, allowing 1 hour for the
small basin and 1¼ to 1½ hours for
the large one. Cool on a wire rack.

Sandwich the cakes together with
a little chocolate icing. Cut to give
5 equal sides. Place on a board and
cover with the remaining icing.

Shape the wafers to make the
cabin door, slide and triangular slide
supports. Press into position, leaving
one side of the cabin open and
beginning the slide at that point.
Invert the cone on top and sprinkle
the coconut around the base to
resemble grass.

Pipe a design on the helter skelter,
using the red icing, and decorate
with smarties and jelly babies.
Makes one 'helter skelter'

80

Football pitch

4-egg Victoria sandwich cake mixture*
250 g (8 oz) green Butter icing (see page 11)
50 g (2 oz) green desiccated coconut (see page 14)
250 g (8 oz) Moulding icing (see page 27)
few drops coffee essence
green food colouring
50 g (2 oz) Glacé icing (see page 9)
3 ice cream wafers
toy football figures

Line and grease two 20 × 30 cm (8 × 12 inch) Swiss roll tins and bake in a preheated moderate oven, 180°C (350°F), Gas Mark 4, for 25 minutes. Turn onto a wire rack to cool.

Sandwich the cakes together with half the butter icing and place on a cake board. Spread the remaining icing over the sides of the cake and coat with the coloured coconut.

Colour a small piece of moulding icing with the coffee essence and shape into a football. Colour the rest green. Roll out on a surface dusted with cornflour to a 20 × 30 cm (8 × 12 inch) rectangle and use to cover the top of the cake.

Using the glacé icing and a No. 2 writing nozzle, pipe white lines on the cake to represent a football pitch. Shape the wafers to make goalposts, fix with a little glacé icing and place at each end of the pitch. Put the players and football in position.
Makes one 'football pitch'

Fire Engine

*6-egg Victoria
    sandwich cake
    mixture**
*350 g (12 oz) red
    Butter icing (see
    note and recipe on
    page 11)*
2 ice cream wafers
*50 g (2 oz) Royal
    icing**
*3 liquorice Catherine
    wheels*
liquorice ribbon
liquorice allsorts
few smarties
*2 sugar bells (see
    page 56)*

diagram 1

diagram 2

diagram 3

diagram 4

Grease and line two 18 × 28 cm (7 × 11 inch) shallow baking tins. Turn the mixture into the tins and bake in a preheated moderate oven, 180°C (350°F), Gas Mark 4, for 30 to 35 minutes. Turn onto a wire rack to cool.

Following diagram 1, cut a 2.5 cm (1 inch) wide strip off the length of each cake; cut each strip into 2 pieces, 18 and 10 cm (7 and 4 inches) long.

Place one cake on a board. Cut two 5 cm (2 inch) pieces off the other cake (see diagram 2), leaving an 18 × 15 cm (7 × 6 inch) piece. Place this piece on the large cake and put the 5 cm (2 inch) strips crosswise on top (see diagram 3).

Place a 10 cm (4 inch) strip on each side, towards the rear. Place the longer strips on top and round off the corners (see diagram 4).

Sandwich all the pieces together with red icing, then cover the cake with the remaining icing. Shape the wafers to make windows and position on the front and sides of the cab.

Put the royal icing into a piping bag, fitted with a No. 2 writing nozzle. Pipe outlines for the windows, doors, wheel hubs etc. as shown.

Position liquorice ribbon for the ladders, radiator grill, bumpers, etc, as shown. Use Catherine wheels for the hoses and liquorice allsorts for the wheels and road markings. Position the sugar bells on top on liquorice sweets, and smarties at the front and back to resemble lights.

Makes one 'fire engine'

NOTE: For a deep red engine, colour the butter icing with edible red paste colouring obtainable from specialist suppliers (see page 95).

Army Tank

4-egg Victoria
  sandwich cake
  mixture*
1 jam Swiss roll
1 wagon wheel
350 g (12 oz) green
  Butter icing (see
  page 11)
few strips liquorice
  ribbon
1 sweet biscuit
small round iced gem
  biscuits
50 g (2 oz) red
  Royal icing*
6 chocolate
  matchmakers
1 sweet cigarette
assorted sweets

Grease and line an 18 cm (7 inch) deep square cake tin. Turn the mixture into the tin and bake in a preheated moderate oven, 160°C (325°F), Gas Mark 3, for 1 hour 15 minutes. Turn onto a wire rack to cool.

Cut a 2.5 cm (1 inch) slice from each side of the cake for the wheel tracks (see diagram 1). Cut a 2.5 cm (1 inch) slice from the end and a 1 cm (½ inch) slice from the bottom of each track (see diagram 2). Cut two 2.5 cm (1 inch) Swiss roll slices, then cut each one in half and attach each end of the tracks with a little icing (see diagram 3).

Shape the cake (see diagram 4) and place on a cake board. Place the wagon wheel on top of the tank. Cut a 5 cm (2 inch) slice of Swiss roll and place on top of the tank slightly towards the rear to represent the turret.

Completely cover the cake with green icing. Cover the wheel tracks and attach to the sides of the cake. Cover the biscuit and stand at the back of the turret to form a lid.

Cut 2 cm (¾ inch) strips of liquorice ribbon and place crosswise at 5 mm (¼ inch) intervals around the wheel tracks. Place the biscuits on the outside of the tracks to represent the drive wheels. Pipe a dot in the centre of each one, using red icing.

Put a toy soldier in the turret. Position 3 chocolate matchmakers on either side of the front to represent the forward guns. Push a sweet cigarette into the front of the turret for the turret gun. Arrange sweets on the tank to represent lights, pipes and peepholes.
Makes one 'army tank'

diagram 1

diagram 2

diagram 3

diagram 4

REFERENCE SECTION

These three recipes have been used for all the cakes in the book. To some extent they are inter-changeable, but for novelty cakes, where shaping is involved, a Victoria sandwich cake is the most suitable.

Victoria Sandwich Cake

This is referred to as a 2-egg mixture. For larger quantities, simply increase the ingredients in proportion.

*125 g (4 oz) butter
  or margarine
125 g (4 oz) caster
  sugar
2 eggs
125 g (4 oz)
  self-raising flour,
  sifted
1 tablespoon hot
  water*

Line and grease the baking tin(s).

Cream the fat and sugar together until light and fluffy. Beat in the eggs one at a time, adding a tablespoon of the flour with the second egg. Fold in the remaining flour with a metal spoon, then the hot water.

Turn the mixture into the prepared tin(s) and bake in a preheated moderate oven, 180°C (350°F), Gas Mark 4, for the required time, until the cake springs back when lightly pressed. Turn onto a wire rack to cool.

VARIATIONS

Chocolate: Blend 1 tablespoon cocoa powder with 1 tablespoon hot water. Cool slightly then beat in with the fat and sugar.

Coffee: Add 1 tablespoon instant coffee powder with the flour.

Orange or Lemon: Add the grated rind of 1 orange or lemon with the fat and sugar. Replace the water with orange or lemon juice.

Pink: Add a few drops of food colouring to the hot water before folding into the mixture.

Whisked Sponge Cake

This is referred to as a 3-egg mixture. For larger quantities, increase the ingredients in proportion.

3 eggs
140 g (4½ oz) caster sugar
75 g (3 oz) plain flour, sifted

Line, grease and flour the baking tin(s).

Place the eggs and sugar in a heatproof bowl over a pan of boiling water and whisk until the mixture is thick and pale and leaves a trail when the whisk is lifted. (The hot water is unnecessary if using an electric beater.)

Fold in the flour with a metal spoon, then turn into the prepared tin(s). Bake in a preheated moderately hot oven, 190°C (375°F), Gas Mark 5, for the required time, until the cake springs back when lightly pressed. Turn onto a wire rack to cool.

VARIATIONS

Chocolate: Replace 25 g (1 oz) flour with cocoa powder; sift with the flour.

Lemon or Orange: Whisk in the grated rind of 1 lemon or orange with the eggs and sugar.

Coffee: Add 1 tablespoon instant coffee powder with the flour.

RICH FRUIT CAKE

For the ingredients, see quantity chart on pages 90-91.

Grease the inside of the tin. Line the base and sides with a double layer of greaseproof paper, allowing it to extend 5 cm (2 inches) above the rim. Grease well. Tie a thick band of newspaper around the outside of the tin. Stand on a pad of newspaper on a baking sheet.

Sift the flour and spices together. Cream the fat and sugar and lemon rind together until light and fluffy. Beat in the treacle. Beat in the eggs one at a time, adding a tablespoon of flour with all but the first. Fold in the remaining flour, the ground almonds, fruit and nuts until thoroughly mixed.

Turn the mixture into the prepared tin(s) and smooth the top with the back of a spoon. Bake on the middle shelf of a preheated cool oven, 140°C (275°F), Gas Mark 1.

Test the smallest 3 cake sizes given in the chart after 3 hours, the larger sizes after 3½ to 4 hours. If a skewer inserted into the centre comes out clean, it is cooked. If not, return the cake to the oven and test again at 30 minute intervals.

Leave in the tin(s) for 30 minutes, then turn onto a wire rack to cool.

Prick the cake with a skewer and spoon the brandy over the surface; this helps to increase the storage time and keeps the cake moist.

Wrap the cake in greaseproof paper and then a double thickness of foil. Store in a cool dry place for 2 to 3 months to mature, before covering with almond paste.

ALMOND PASTE

For the ingredients see the quantity chart on pages 90-91.

Mix the almonds and sugars together in a mixing bowl and make a well in the centre. Add the lemon juice, almond essence and enough egg yolk or beaten egg to mix to a firm paste.

Turn onto a surface sprinkled with icing sugar and knead lightly until smooth; do not over-knead or the paste will become oily and difficult to handle. Keep in a polythene bag until required as almond paste dries out quickly if exposed to air.

Note: When a recipe calls for a given quantity of paste, e.g. Simnel Cake, this is the total weight of the paste. To obtain the weight required use half ground almonds to a quarter each icing and caster sugar.

Ready-made Almond Paste or Marzipan

This can be used instead of home-made almond paste for convenience, although it does not have quite the same flavour. To obtain the amount required for a certain sized cake, simply add the weight of the ground almonds and sugars given in the almond paste chart for that cake size.

ROYAL ICING

For the ingredients, see the quantity chart on pages 90-91.

Beat the egg whites with a fork until frothy. Gradually beat in half the icing sugar, using a wooden spoon. Beat in half the remaining icing sugar with the glycerine, if using, and lemon juice. Beat thoroughly until smooth and white. Beat in enough of the remaining icing sugar to give a consistency that stands in soft peaks. Add colouring if required.

Cover the bowl with a damp cloth and leave to stand for several hours to allow any air bubbles to rise to the surface and burst. Before using stir well with a wooden spoon; do not overbeat.

If using an electric mixer, use on the slowest speed and leave the icing to stand for 24 hours as it will incorporate more air which needs longer to disperse. If air pockets are not dispersed, they will cause breaks in the icing during piping.

Note: If a recipe calls for a given quantity of royal icing, this refers to the amount of icing sugar used. For each 250 g (8 oz) icing sugar, 1 egg white is required.

Using Royal Icing

The required consistency of royal icing depends upon its use. For flat icing or piping rosettes it should be fairly firm. For piping lattice work or writing it should be a little thinner. For run-outs it will need to be thinned with a little lightly beaten egg white to flood the shapes.

Quantity Chart for Rich Fruit Cake

Round	15 cm (6 inch)	18 cm (7 inch)	20 cm (8 inch)
Square	13 cm (5 inch)	15 cm (6 inch)	18 cm (7 inch)
Plain flour	125 g (4 oz)	175 g (6 oz)	200 g (7 oz)
Ground mixed spice	½ teaspoon	½ teaspoon	1 teaspoon
Ground nutmeg	good pinch	½ teaspoon	½ teaspoon
Butter or margarine	100 g (3½ oz)	150 g (5 oz)	175 g (6 oz)
Soft brown sugar	100 g (3½ oz)	150 g (5 oz)	175 g (6 oz)
Grated lemon rind	½ lemon	1 lemon	1 lemon
Black treacle	½ tablespoon	1 tablespoon	1 tablespoon
Eggs	2 large	3 large	4 large
Ground almonds	25 g (1 oz)	40 g (1½ oz)	50 g (2 oz)
Currants	175 g (6 oz)	250 g (8 oz)	300 g (10 oz)
Sultanas	125 g (4 oz)	150 g (5 oz)	200 g (7 oz)
Raisins	50 g (2 oz)	75 g (3 oz)	125 g (4 oz)
Glacé cherries	40 g (1½ oz)	50 g (2 oz)	65 g (2½ oz)
Mixed peel	40 g (1½ oz)	50 g (2 oz)	65 g (2½ oz)
Blanched almonds	40 g (1½ oz)	50 g (2 oz)	65 g (2½ oz)
Brandy	1 tablespoon	1 tablespoon	2 tablespoons

Quantity Chart for Almond Paste

Round	15 cm (6 inch)	18 cm (7 inch)	20 cm (8 inch)
Square	13 cm (5 inch)	15 cm (6 inch)	18 cm (7 inch)
Ground almonds	175 g (6 oz)	250 g (8 oz)	350 g (12 oz)
Caster sugar	75 g (3 oz)	125 g (4 oz)	175 g (6 oz)
Icing sugar	75 g (3 oz)	125 g (4 oz)	175 g (6 oz)
Lemon juice	1 teaspoon	1 teaspoon	2 teaspoons
Almond essence	2 drops	2 drops	3 drops
Eggs	1 yolk	1 standard	1 standard

Quantity Chart for Royal Icing

Round	15 cm (6 inch)	18 cm (7 inch)	20 cm (8 inch)
Square	13 cm (5 inch)	15 cm (6 inch)	18 cm (7 inch)
Egg whites	2	2	3
Icing sugar	500 g (1 lb)	575 g (1¼ lb)	675 g (1½ lb)
Lemon juice	1 teaspoon	1 teaspoon	1 teaspoon
Glycerine (optional)	1 teaspoon	1 teaspoon	1½ teaspoons

These quantities are sufficient for applying two coats of royal icing and simple decoration.

3 cm (9 inch)	25 cm (10 inch)	28 cm (11 inch)	30 cm (12 inch)
0 cm (8 inch)	23 cm (9 inch)	25 cm (10 inch)	28 cm (11 inch)
75 g (9 oz)	325 g (11 oz)	400 g (14 oz)	500 g (1 lb)
½ teaspoons	2 teaspoons	2 teaspoons	2 teaspoons
2 teaspoon	½ teaspoon	½ teaspoon	1 teaspoon
50 g (8 oz)	300 g (10 oz)	350 g (12 oz)	400 g (14 oz)
50 g (8 oz)	300 g (10 oz)	350 g (12 oz)	400 g (14 oz)
lemon	1 lemon	2 lemons	2 lemons
tablespoon	2 tablespoons	2 tablespoons	2 tablespoons
large	6 large	7 large	8 large
5 g (2½ oz)	75 g (3 oz)	100 g (3½ oz)	125 g (4 oz)
75 g (13 oz)	500 g (1 lb)	575 g (1¼ lb)	675 g (1½ lb)
75 g (9 oz)	325 g (11 oz)	375 g (13 oz)	500 g (1 lb)
50 g (5 oz)	175 g (6 oz)	200 g (7 oz)	250 g (8 oz)
00 g (3½ oz)	125 g (4 oz)	150 g (5 oz)	175 g (6 oz)
00 g (3½ oz)	125 g (4 oz)	150 g (5 oz)	175 g (6 oz)
00 g (3½ oz)	125 g (4 oz)	150 g (5 oz)	175 g (6 oz)
tablespoons	3 tablespoons	3 tablespoons	4 tablespoons

3 cm (9 inch)	25 cm (10 inch)	28 cm (11 inch)	30 cm (12 inch)
0 cm (8 inch)	23 cm (9 inch)	25 cm (10 inch)	28 cm (11 inch)
00 g (1 lb)	575 g (1¼ lb)	675 g (1½ lb)	800 g (1¾ lb)
50 g (8 oz)	300 g (10 oz)	350 g (12 oz)	400 g (14 oz)
50 g (8 oz)	300 g (10 oz)	350 g (12 oz)	400 g (14 oz)
2 teaspoons	3 teaspoons	3 teaspoons	4 teaspoons
drops	½ teaspoon	½ teaspoon	1 teaspoon
large	2 large	2 large + 1 yolk	3 large

23 cm (9 inch)	25 cm (10 inch)	28 cm (11 inch)	30 cm (12 inch)	
20 cm (8 inch)	23 cm (9 inch)	25 cm (10 inch)	28 cm (11 inch)	
3	4	4	5	
00 g (2 lb)	1 kg (2¼ lb)	1.25 kg (2½ lb)	1.5 kg (3 lb)	
2 teaspoons	2 teaspoons	2 teaspoons	3 teaspoons	
½ teaspoons	2 teaspoons	2 teaspoons	3 teaspoons	

DECORATION TEMPLATES

INDEX